TO DO WID ME

BENJAMIN ZEPHANIAH
TO DO WID ME

BENJAMIN ZEPHANIAH FILMED LIVE & DIRECT
BY PAMELA ROBERTSON-PEARCE

BLOODAXE BOOKS

ISBN: 978 1 85224 943 4

First published in 2013 by
Bloodaxe Books Ltd,
Highgreen,
Tarset,
Northumberland NE48 1RP,

www.bloodaxebooks.com
For further information about Bloodaxe titles
please visit our website or write to
the above address for a catalogue.

Supported using public funding by
**ARTS COUNCIL
ENGLAND**

Cover design: Neil Astley & Pamela Robertson-Pearce.

Printed in Great Britain by
Bell & Bain Limited, Glasgow, Scotland.

CONTENTS

Benjamin Zephaniah: To Do Wid Me
a film by Pamela Robertson-Pearce

12   Naked   (Brunel University)

16   Man to Man   (Brunel University)

17   I Love Me Mother   (Birmingham)

18   Drivosaurus Rex   (Keats House)

19   Who's Who   (Keats House)

20   No Problem   (Keats House)

21   I Have a Scheme   (Ledbury)

24   Dis policeman is kicking me to death   (Brunel University)

27   What Stephen Lawrence Has Taught Us   (Lincolnshire)

29   Dis Poetry   (Live Theatre, Newcastle)

31   Wake Up   (Lincolnshire)

34   Meditate and Communicate   (Brunel University)

36   Rong Radio   (Beta Brothers music video, London)

39   Football Mad   (Keats House)

41   Money   (Live Theatre, Newcastle)

45   Talking Turkeys   (Keats House)

47   To Do Wid Me   (Birmingham)

51   Nu Run Away   (Birmingham)

BONUS: **Benjamin Zephaniah music videos**
by The Beta Brothers & Mango Island

54   Us & Dem   (Mango Island)

57   Touch   (Beta Brothers)

60   Responsible   (Beta Brothers)

62   Genetics   (Beta Brothers)

To Do Wid Me: credits

SPECIAL THANKS TO
Benjamin Zephaniah
Valerie Wright
Zane Springer

DIRECTOR
Pamela Robertson-Pearce

PRODUCER
Neil Astley

CAMERA
Pamela Robertson-Pearce

FILM EDITED BY
Neil Astley
Pamela Robertson-Pearce

ADDITIONAL FILMING
Neil Astley
Joe Chapman
Alan Sennett
The Beta Brothers

RONG RADIO
by The Beta Brothers
www.thebetabrothers.com

MUSIC
Belly of De Beast
Produced & mixed by the Mad Professor
Ariwa Music © 1996

ADRIAN MITCHELL
'Most people' from
Come On Everybody: Poems 1953-2008
published by Bloodaxe Books

POEMS FROM

The Dread Affair (1985)
published by Arena

City Psalms (1992)
Propa Propaganda (1996)
Too Black Too Strong (2001)
published by Bloodaxe Books

Talking Turkeys (1994)
Funky Chickens (1996)
Wicked World (2000)
published by Puffin Books

THANKS TO
Arts Council England
Brunel University
English & Media Centre, London
Keats House, London
Betty Layward Primary School, London
Ledbury Poetry Festival
Live Theatre, Newcastle
Midland Creative Projects, Birmingham
Queen's Hall, Hexham
Paul Batchelor
Jonathan Davidson
Chloe Garner
Dave Maughan
Maureen Roberts
Michael Simons

BONUS FEATURE: MUSIC VIDEOS
Directed & edited by The Beta Brothers
www.thebetabrothers.com
'Us an Dem' by Mango Island
MUSIC: *Naked* 2005
One Little Indian Ltd
www.littleindian.co.uk
copyright © Benjamin Zephaniah

To Do Wid Him: The Man, the Poet, the Film

Foreword by NEIL ASTLEY

Benjamin Obadiah Iqbal Zephaniah is an oral poet, novelist, playwright, children's writer and reggae artist; he has been a political activist, a Rastafarian and a vegan since his teens. Born in 1958 in Birmingham, he grew up in the Handsworth part of the city ('the Jamaican capital of Europe'), from where he was sent to an 'approved school' for being uncontrollable and rebellious. One teacher branded him 'a born failure', as you'll hear in this film. Years later he learned that he was dyslexic.

His mother Valerie came from Jamaica (where Benjamin spent some of his childhood), and found employment in Britain as a nurse. He has eight brothers and sisters and is one of a pair of twins. His father was Barbadian and worked for the Post Office, a connection which proved problematical when Valerie left him after years of abuse, taking Benjamin with her and trying to stay untraced. The first person he stood up for in his life was his mother; when he was big enough, he'd intervene to protect her.

At 13, he was on the streets, unable to read and write, and fell in with other disaffected black youths, ending up in borstal (youth prison) and later jail for burglary and affray (rioting). But all this time he was writing poems, composing them in his head and learning them by heart; and it was through poetry, music and political activism that he found his vocation and subject.

His coming of age happened at a time of great social unrest in Britain: economic recession, industrial conflict, high unemployment (especially among black youths), poor housing, homelessness and racial discrimination, all fuelling numerous demonstrations. On the streets of Birmingham, London and other major cities, police using the notorious 'sus' laws of stop and search inflamed feelings in the black community. Social and economic deprivation during the 1980s, coupled with widespread resentment against the police, sparked riots in Handsworth, Bristol, London, Leeds, Liverpool and elsewhere, while in the coalfields riot police enforced Margaret Thatcher's crushing of the Miners' Strike. Benjamin soon became involved with a number of protests, and over the years has championed many causes, from the Anti-Apartheid Movement to the campaigns for justice by relatives of the murdered teenager Stephen Lawrence (killed in 1993) and of Benjamin's own cousin Mikey Powell (who died in police custody in 2003). He is a patron of many organisations, including the Vegan Society, the Palestine Solidarity Campaign, and Inquest (a charity which helps people bereaved following contentious deaths, particularly deaths in custody), and groups working with young people and in community centres, women's refuges and prisons.

While still a teenager in Birmingham he started to build a following for his timely poetry – political poems, lyrics for songs and 'dub poetry', words spoken over a reggae instrumental track in the manner of Jamaican 'toaster' DJs. But with friends killed in street violence, or sent to prison for life, and himself endangered (sleeping with a handgun under his pillow), he reached his make-or-break moment, and left Birmingham for London. There he started performing his poetry at music venues while unsuccessfully hawking his work around the publishers. His publishing break came when he discovered Page One, a community bookshop and café in East London, where he joined the cooperative and helped to produce his first book of poems, *Pen Rhythm*, in 1980.

His second collection, *The Dread Affair*, was published by Hutchinson's short-lived Arena imprint in 1985, but was out of print – and largely out of favour with the author – when I approached him after a reading at Newcastle Arts Centre in the early 90s and asked him if he had a publisher for all the new work he was then performing. He has since published three collections with Bloodaxe, *City Psalms* (1992), *Propa Propaganda* (1996) and *Too Black Too Strong* (2001), the latter including poems written while working with Michael Mansfield QC and other Tooks barristers on the Stephen Lawrence case.

Benjamin established himself as a writer through his live performances of 'political, musical, radical poetry' at music venues and festivals, but was able to make a much greater impact when he started being asked to perform on television. He has said that his mission was to take poetry everywhere; he hated the 'dead image that academia and the establishment had given poetry' and he wanted 'to popularise poetry by reaching people who did not read books'.

Later, he was able to reach younger readers and audiences. As well as Benjamin Zephaniah the writer of forthright poetry with a political edge for adults, there's also Benjamin Zephaniah the children's poet, known for his poetry with attitude for children, with massively popular collections like *Talking Turkeys* (1994), *Funky Chickens* (1996) and *Wicked World* (2000), all from Puffin/Penguin. The reasons for his popularity as a children's writer are clear from the film. Performing for and engaging with a class of London school children visiting Keats House, he doesn't patronise or talk down to them, and he doesn't shirk from addressing difficult issues in his poems or comments: racism, dyslexia, bullying, youth crime and capitalism. A poem about dinosaurs and *Jurassic Park* is also a playful satire on commercial merchandising, while other poems question footballers' pay and the cost of the NASA space programme. Many of his children's poems are about animals, but as a vegan he feels obliged to remind all readers that today's farm animals are tomorrow's slabs of meat at the butcher's which in turn become the Sunday joint on the dinner table. His reading at Keats House ends with his best-known children's poem, the subversive 'Talking Turkeys', in which 'turkeys jus wanna hav fun… Turkeys are cool, an turkeys are wicked / An every turkey has a Mum.'

Readers of all ages have been inspired by Benjamin's example of someone who managed to turn his life around despite social disadvantages and poor education, becoming a respected writer and role model. Another challenge he has taken on is writing gritty novels for teenagers. These have proved that difficult teenage boys can be persuaded to read books if they feel they can relate to the characters and identify with what they are going through in their lives. The first of these, *Face* (1999), was followed by *Refugee Boy* (2001), *Gangsta Rap* (2004) and *Teacher's Dead* (2007), all from Bloomsbury. And he has published two provocative anthologies for teenage readers with AK Press, *Schools Out: Poems Not for School* (1997) and *The Little Book of Vegan Poems* (2001) with a warning on the cover: *explicit vegan lyrics*.

Benjamin also has his own reggae band, which takes to the road when he feels it's time to do another music tour. He has produced numerous recordings, including *Dub Ranting* (1982), *Rasta* (1983), *Us an Dem* (1990), *Back to Roots* (1995), *Belly of de Beast* (1996) and *Naked* (2004). Some of these have been promoted with music videos, one of which, 'Rong Radio', is included in the film, with another four added as a bonus feature on the DVD. He was the first person to record with the Wailers after the death of Bob Marley, in a musical tribute to Nelson Mandela, which Mandela heard while in prison on Robben Island. Their later meetings led to Benjamin working with children in South African townships and hosting the President's Two Nations Concert at the Royal Albert Hall in 1996. He has recorded with many different artists, including Dennis Bovell, Kinobe, Amira Saqati, Sinead O'Connor, Mieko Shimizu, and Swayzak.

In 1989 he was nominated for Oxford Professor of Poetry, and has since received honorary doctorates from sixteen universities, but famously refused to accept a nomination in 2003 for an OBE – the Queen's Order of the British Empire – because he saw it as a status symbol of Britain's colonial past. He was voted Britain's third favourite poet of all time (after T.S. Eliot and John Donne) in a BBC poll in 2009.

In 2006 he moved out of London to Lincolnshire, and for some years has spent part of each year in China, studying martial arts including tai chi. In 2011 he was poet-in-residence at Keats House, before making a radical career change by taking up his first-ever academic position as Chair in Creative Writing at Brunel University in West London, with a brief to work with students on performance poetry.

Rare – indeed unique – among poets, Benjamin Zephaniah has become a household name. He has appeared in a number of television programmes, including *Eastenders*, *The Bill*, *Live and Kicking*, *Blue Peter* and *Wise Up*, and played Gower in a BBC Radio 3 production of Shakespeare's *Pericles* in 2005. He can't walk down the street without being stopped by people who want his autograph or want to tell him how much his poetry or his books have meant to them, or just to talk. Even the traffic police, who pull him over regularly (still the racial profiling: a Rasta driving a fancy car?), now respond with embarrassment not intimidation when he rolls down the window: 'Bloody 'ell, it's the poet!' exclaimed a surprised officer on one of these occasions. Everyone thinks they know him, but often they're only familiar with one aspect of his life or work.

When we first talked about making a film with Benjamin, we especially wanted to capture some of his live performances, but having known him for many years, we quickly realised that a much more creative challenge would be to try to show as many sides as possible of this man of many parts – and how all those parts come together in *one love, one heart, one world*. As well as filming five live performances with different kinds of audiences, we interviewed Benjamin at his home in Lincolnshire and with his mother Valerie in Birmingham (and with nephew Zane).

In editing our footage over many months, we kept picking up more and more connections and recurrent threads in the performances, discussions and interactions we had filmed at various times over four years. The narrative Pamela has created draws these out in such a way that this is a film which can be appreciated not just once but with repeated viewings. She also made the decision that all the poems and songs included in the film – twenty in total – would be heard and seen in full; unlike in most film portraits, none would be cut or excerpted; and all the words or lyrics are included in the book of the film.

Over the years Benjamin has made changes to some of the poems when performing them. The versions included in this book are those he now performs on stage – as captured in the film – and differ in places from the original published texts.

Afterword by PAMELA ROBERTSON–PEARCE

I just want to add a few words about the making of *To Do Wid Me*. From start to finish this has been a pleasurable experience. This has everything to do with Benjamin and Neil, a great team to work with. I have been very fortunate in that Neil has been completely supportive of me as a filmmaker, and as a producer and film editor he has been superb. In dealing with Benjamin as a subject I have got to know a person who walks the walk and talks the talk. He is not only completely professional but also relaxed, friendly and flexible; not encumbered by an ego, he adapts easily. He is a delight to work with and to be around.

Another person I am very grateful to have met through this film is Valerie Wright. I liked her instantly. She has a great spirit. I can tell that having a mother like her who is in your corner no matter what and who believes in you, is part of what makes Benjamin who he is. In my mind I dedicate this film to Valerie, for without her Benjamin would not be here today. I also want to thank Zane Springer for allowing his uncle Benj to win in their backyard soccer match.

Naked

Dis is me naked. Unclothed, undressed under
    the light of all the Gods that you dare
    imagine, waiting to be touched with as
    many versions of the truth as you
    can conjure up in your turned off mind

Dis is me. Give me your theory, give me
    your opinion, give me your truth, give me
    your big bad holy book, let me know
    exactly what tried and tested faith
    keeps you asleep.

Dis is me, hungry for the priceless forbidden, looking
    for the man who wrote the superhighway code
    so that I can rob his richness.
    He got insurance, he got the state, let me get him.
    I wanna find game show hosts and put
    the bastards on trial. I wanna kill educated ignorance.

Dis is me naked, revolting in front of you, I'm
    not much but I give a damn. Lovers look
    at me, haters look at me as I exhibit
    my love and my fury on dis desperate stage

Dis is me naked. I love being naked.
    I look at my naked self and I know
    that I was made for nakedness. I see
    my neighbours naked, I see booted and
    suited men naked, and women in purdah
    naked, and all the priests and politicians
    who I despise are naked looking
    at the truth, facing reality, having to
    deal with themselves, by themselves. Praise
    the Gods for the black, brown, white, fat,

thin, one-legged, blind, bent and uneven
naked bodies. Praise the female Gods
and the older Gods for the naked body
beautiful.

Dis is my mother. She read a poster on a
hot tin street in Jamaica that told her
that Britain loves her. She tuned
into the dream that made me the
naked cop beater that I
am today. I do all dis stuff for my
mother and she cries because I will
not go to church.

Dis is me naked, jealous, passionate, listening
for the naked sound of liberty,
waiting for the militants to arise, pouring
the lubricant sweat into the system
of rebellion.

Dis is me invading the blank page with my
endless aerodynamic pen, driven like
optimistic hope, driven, raging,
desperate, hungry, inspired by the
chit-chat overheard on stinky smoky buses
turned on by the politics of the kitchen.

Dis is me. Dreadlocks I. Rastafari. Rastafari.
Behold, how good and how pleasant
it is for revolutionaries to dwell together
in the house of the lord. Knowing that
the real God will liberate those who liberate
themselves I shall fear no religion.
Took away the dried up intermediary, got
a direct line to the great ganja
creator. Dis is me, Rastafari, Rastafari,
Dreadlocks I.

Dis is me blowing my lonely black trumpet.

Dis is me mysteriously trying to smile, trying
        to convince myself that dis is the
        lesser of evils. I stagger from
        column to column stealing from its
        stolen concrete as I go. 'Fall Babylon,
        Fall Babylon and take your bankers
        with you,' I chant as I piss on parliament.

Dis is me, standing under understanding,
        getting up and over, overstanding the
        corruption of our role models. The
        lack of courage of our athletes burns me.

Dis is my music. Loud, deep, Jungle music.
        Heavy, roots, Reggae dub stuff.
        I rave like a lover, I love like a raver
        I know it's only Hip-Hop Rock but I like it,
        I'm so proud of it. We rocked the world
        with it. We turned on generations
        with it, made love and riots with
        it, we created the magic
        but we still don't own the magic.
        Why must we still struggle for our royalty cheque?

Dis is me fatherless, childless. Who do I go to and for what?
        Who shall I cry to? Who shall I cry for?
        I need babies to recite to
        I need babies to recite to me
        my life is full of lonely childless eternities
        where only poetry gives me life
        and nakedness gives me knowledge.
        When I cry they want to arrest me, when I'm in
        need I'm suspicious, when I cross the road
        they ask me why.

Dis is me. I hate dis government as much as I
    hated the one before it and I have reason
    to believe that I will hate the one to come.

Dis is me, squeeze me. Let me free me.
    I have come to realise that what you can do for me
    I can do much better for me.
    Let me do for my loved ones what you will not do for them
    I want to hold the hands of my loved ones
    (Those who have no one to vote for)
    and cause a victorious rumble in dis black universe.
    I am naked, whispering screams in the church
    of the impatient revolutionaries. I may be
    vulnerable, I may not have the education of my critics or
    the wealth of my arresting officers, but I have
    never felt the need to wear a uniform in order
    to break laws and I have never felt the need to
    eat dead bodies in order to feel like a good human.

FILM: Brunel University, 15 March 2012
POEM: *Too Black Too Strong* (Bloodaxe Books, 2001)

Man to Man

Macho man
Can't cook
Macho man
Can't sew
Macho man
Eats plenty Red Meat,
At home him is King,
From front garden to back garden
From de lift to de balcony
Him a supreme Master,
Controller.

Food mus ready
On time,
Cloth mus ready
On time,
Woman mus ready
On time,
How Macho can yu go?

Cum
Talk to me bout sexuality,
Cum meditate,
Cum Save de Whale,
Dose bulging muscles need Tai Chi
Yu drunken eyes need herb tea,
Cum, Relax.

Macho man
Can't cook, sew or wash him pants,
But Macho Man is in full control.

FILM: Brunel University, 15 March 2012
POEM: *City Psalms* (Bloodaxe Books, 1992)

I Love Me Mudder

I luv me mudder and me mudder luvs me
  We cum so far from over de sea,
We heard dat de streets were paved wid gold
  Sometimes it's hot, sometime it's cold,
I luv me mudder and me mudder luvs me
  We try fe live in harmony
Yu might know her as Valerie
  But to me she's just my mummy.

She shouts at me daddy so loud sometime
  She's always been a friend of mine
She's always doing de best she can
  She works so hard down ina Englan,
She's always singin sum kinda song
  She has big muscles an she very, very strong,
She likes pussycats an she luvs cashew nuts
  An she don't bother wid no ifs and buts.

I luv me mudder and me mudder luvs me
  We cum so far from over de sea,
We heard dat de streets were paved wid gold
  Sometimes it's hot, sometime it's cold,
I luv her and whatever we do
  Dis is a luv I know is true,
My people, I'm talking to yu
  Me and my mudder we luv you too.

FILM: Birmingham, 17 July 2012
POEM: *Wicked World* (Puffin Books, 2000)

Drivosaurus Rex

The dinosaurs are back
Working at Hollywood
Now they are not flesh and bone
They're plastic, foam and wood
The dinosaurs are here
I saw one on a bus
As I was on the way to play
At Dinosaurs 'R' Us.

They came from Noah's Ark
Unto Jurassic Park
When they eat you can bet
They did some great big
Barks,
Then from Jurassic Park
Some came into our homes
In big boxes of cereals
With added rocks and stones.

The dinosaurs are back
With bottom, front and side
The ones I've seen look kind of mean
And really very wide,
These dinosaurs are stars
I've seen them on radars
Looking cool and deadly
As they drive around in cars.

FILM: Keats House, 12 October 2011
POEM: *Talking Turkeys* (Puffin Books, 1994/1995)

Who's Who

I used to think nurses
Were women,
I used to think police
Were men,
I used to think poets
Were boring,
Until I became one of them.

FILM: Keats House, 12 October 2011
POEM: *Talking Turkeys* (Puffin Books, 1994/1995)

No Problem

I am not de problem
But I bear de brunt
Of silly playground taunts
An racist stunts,
I am not de problem
I am a born academic
But dey got me on de run
Now I am branded athletic,
I am not de problem
If yu give I a chance
I can teach yu of Timbuktu
I can do more dan dance,
I am not de problem
I greet yu wid a smile
Yu put me in a pigeon hole
But I am versatile.

These conditions may affect me
As I get older,
An I am positively sure
I hav no chips on me shoulders,
Black is not de problem
Mother country get it right,
An juss fe de record,
Sum of me best friends are white.

FILM: Keats House, 12 October 2011
POEM: *Propa Propaganda* (Bloodaxe Books, 1996)

I Have a Scheme

I am here today my friends to tell you there is hope
As high as that mountain may seem
I must tell you
I have a dream
And my friends
There is a tunnel at the end of the light.
And beyond that tunnel I see a future
I see a time
When angry white men
Will sit down with angry black women
And talk about the weather,
Black employers will display notice-boards proclaiming,
'Me nu care wea yu come from yu know
So long as yu can do a good day's work, dat cool wid me.'

I see a time
When words like affirmative action
Will have sexual connotations
And black people all over this blessed country of ours
Will play golf,
Yes my friends that time is coming
And in that time
Afro-Caribbean and Asian youth
Will spend big money on English takeaways
And all police officers will be armed
With a dumplin,
I see a time
A time when the President of the United States of America
        will stand up and say,
'I inhaled
And it did kinda nice
So rewind and cum again.'
Immigration officers will just check that you are all right
And all black people will speak Welsh.

I may not get there my friends
But I have seen that time
I see thousands of muscular black men on Hampstead Heath walking
        their poodles
And hundreds of black female Formula 1 drivers
Racing around Birmingham in pursuit of a truly British way of life.
I have a dream
That one day from all the churches of this land we will hear the sound
        of that great old English spiritual,
Here we go, Here we go, Here we go.
One day all great songs will be made that way.

I am here today my friends to tell you
That the time is coming
When all people, regardless of gender, colour or class, will have at least
        one Barry Manilow record
And vending-machines throughout the continent of Europe
Will flow with sour sap and sugarcane juice,
For it is written in the great book of multiculturalism
That the curry will blend with the shepherd's pie
And the Afro hairstyle will return.

Let me hear you say
Multiculture
Amen
Let me hear you say
Roti, Roti
A women.

The time is coming
I may not get there with you
But I have seen that time,
And as an Equal Opportunities poet
It pleases me
To give you this opportunity

To share my vision of hope
And I just hope you can cope
With a future as black as this.

FILM: Ledbury Poetry Festival, 11 July 2009
POEM: *Propa Propaganda* (Bloodaxe Books, 1996)

Dis policeman keeps on kicking me to death

Ina de distance of de night
you see dem moving round
investigating and crime-making
within any town,
creeping persons wid no hearts
dem control who dem please
dem only like fe see you
when you do pon youn bending knees.
Some of us will fight dem, we fight dem
some of us fight back
informers will sleep wid you
dem stab you ina yu back
dis regime is racist we know
dis regime is bent
dis regime is like a worthless penny
dat's unspent.

Dis policeman keeps on hitting me and pulling out my locks
he keeps on feeding me unlimited Brocklax
dis policeman is a coward he gets me from behind
he can jail my body but him cannot jail my mind.

Like a bat from hell he comes at night
to work his evil plan
although he goes to church on Sunday
he's a sinner man,
like a thief in de dark he take me to de
place where he just left
and when him get me in der
he is kicking me to death.
Dis policeman, dis policeman
dis policeman keeps on kicking me to death.

I got me up and took me to de place fe human rights
a notice on de door said 'Sorry we are closed tonight'
so I turn round and took myself to see dis preacher guy
who told me 'bout some heaven
dat was in de bloody sky,
now I don't wa' to kid myself
but I don't think I'm free
if I'm free den why does he
keep fucking kicking me?

I tell you I'm not joking
you should see dem over der
dey have no respect for either
living or welfare,
dis policeman is a creep
I tell you he is mad
I am trying to do good
while he exhibits bad.
I am living in de ghetto
trying to do my best
when dis policeman tells me
I'm under damn arrest.

Him beat me so badly
I was on the floor
him said if I don't plead guilty
him gwan kick me more
I was feeling sick, I pleaded
RACIST ATTACK
and another policeman come to finish me off –
dis one was BLACK.

In dis war we have traitors
who don't think to sell you out
in dis war der are people who refuse
to hear de shout

for human rights to be regarded
as a basic right
still dis policeman dicks me
every day and every night.

Like a bat from hell he comes at night
to work his evil plan
although he goes to church on Sunday
he's a sinner man
like a thief in de dark he takes me to
de place where he just left
and when him get me in der
he is kicking me to death.
Dis policeman, dis policeman
dis policeman keeps on kicking me to death.

FILM: Brunel University, 16 March 2012
POEM: *The Dread Affair* (Arena, 1985)

What Stephen Lawrence Has Taught Us

We know who the killers are,
We have watched them strut before us
As proud as sick Mussolinis.
We have watched them strut before us
Compassionless and arrogant,
They paraded before us,
Like angels of death
Protected by the law.

It is now an open secret
Black people do not have
Chips on their shoulders,
They just have injustice on their backs
And justice on their minds,
And now we know that the road to liberty
Is as long as the road from slavery.

The death of Stephen Lawrence
Has taught us to love each other
And never to take the tedious task
Of waiting for a bus for granted.
Watching his parents watching the cover-up
Begs the question
What are the trading standards here?
Why are we paying for a police force
That will not work for us?

The death of Stephen Lawrence
Has taught us
That we cannot let the illusion of freedom
Endow us with a false sense of security as we walk the streets,
The whole world can now watch
The academics and the super cops
Struggling to define institutionalised racism

As we continue to die in custody
As we continue emptying our pockets on the pavements,
And we continue to ask ourselves
Why is it so official
That black people are so often killed
Without killers?

We are not talking about war or revenge
We are not talking about hypothetics or possibilities,
We are talking about where we are now
We are talking about how we live now
In dis state
Under dis flag (God Save the Queen),
And God save all those black children who want to grow up
And God save all the brothers and sisters
Who like raving,
Because the death of Stephen Lawrence
Has taught us that racism is easy when
You have friends in high places.
And friends in high places
Have no use whatsoever
When they are not your friends.

Dear Mr Condon,
Pop out of Teletubby land,
And visit reality,
Come to an honest place
And get some advice from your neighbours,
Be enlightened by our community,
Neglect your well-paid ignorance
Because
We know who the killers are.

FILM: Lincolnshire, 17 March 2012
POEM: *Too Black Too Strong* (Bloodaxe Books, 2001)

Dis Poetry

Dis poetry is like a riddim dat drops
De tongue shoots a riddim dat shoots like shots
Dis poetry is designed fe rantin
Dance hall style, Big mouth chanting,
Dis poetry won't put yu to sleep
Saying follow me
Like yu're blind sheep,
Dis poetry is not Party Political
Not designed fe dose who are critical.

Dis poetry is wid me when I gu to me bed
It gets into my Dreadlocks
It lingers around my head
Dis poetry goes wid me as I riding my bike
I've tried Shakespeare, Respect due dere
But dis is de stuff I like.

Dis poetry is not afraid of going ina book
No, but dis poetry need ears to hear an eyes to hav a look
Yes, dis poetry is Verbal Riddim, no big words involved
An if I hav a problem de riddim gets it solved,
I've tried to be Romantic, it does nu good for me
I tek a Reggae Riddim an build my poetry,
I could try something personal
But you've heard it all before,
No written words not needed
Cause many words in store,
Dis poetry is called Dub Ranting
De tongue plays a beat
An de body starts skanking,
Dis poetry is quick an childish
Dis poetry is fe de wise an foolish,
Anybody can do it fe free,
Dis poetry is fe yu an me,

Don't stretch yu imagination
Dis poetry is fe de good of de Nation,
Chant,
In de morning
I chant
In de night
I chant
In de darkness
An under de spotlight,
I pass thru University
I pass thru Sociology
An den I got a Dread degree
In Dreadfull Ghettology.
Dis poetry is wid me when I take a walk
An when I am talking to meself in poetry I talk,
Dis poetry is wid me,
Below me
An above,
Yu see
Dis poetry's from inside me
An goes to yu
WID LUV.

FILM: Live Theatre, Newcastle, 15 March 2009
POEM: *City Psalms* (Bloodaxe Books, 1992)

Wake Up

Wake up, wake up, wake up, Arise.
Wake up, wake up, wake up, Arise.

You hav your money
Your colour TV
Your mobility
Your big salary
You hav your ID
You own all you see now –
Wake up from your sleep.

You're big wid de boss
You made up de loss
You bow to de cross
You're still into Bros.
You're not into us
You don't give a toss now –
Wake up from your sleep.

Cause all yu do is slumber
    yu nu work intelligently.
You may know yu name and number
    but yu live de fantasy.
Yes all yu a do is nothing,
    and nothing will not do.
Sometime you muss do something,
    or something will do you.

You fly every year
You just bought a share
You hav greasy hair
You hav a home spare
You fear despair
You just don't care now –
Wake up from your sleep.

Your mortgage is cool
Your kids luv school
You make every rule
Your home has a pool
Run on green fuel
You're playing de fool now –
Wake up from your sleep.

Cause all yu a do is exist,
   and de time has come to live.
Come out dat big mist
   and practise how to give.
Yes all yu want is status,
   den yu put dat wid a quo.
If yu wake up now yu may
   just live good before you go.

You pay your way
Work, rest and play
You plan your day
You plan your stay
Cause come what may
You'll be ok now –
Wake up from your sleep.

As cool as ice
You drink wid pol lice
You may for advice
You don't mind de price
Cause life is so nice
And you don't live twice now –
Wake up from your sleep yeah.

(BREAK)

Wake up from your sleep.
(repeat)

Cause all yu do is follow,
    you come in like lost sheep.
Some time before tomorrow
    you must wake up from your sleep.
Yes all you a do is conform
    believing you are free.
What you see as de norm
    is normal insanity.

You have your pension plan
You have your wages in your hand
Your bills are paid upon demand now –
Wake up from your sleep.

Your partner's at home cooking
You think you're not bad looking
Big Brother has your booking now –
Wake up from your sleep yeah.

(TROMBONE SOLO)

Wake up from your sleep
Wake up from your sleep
Wake up from your sleep
Wake up from your sleep
Wake up from your sleep

FILM: Lincolnshire, 17 March 2012
MUSIC & LYRICS: *Belly of De Beast* (Ariwa Music, 1996)

Meditate and Communicate

A Sadhu
Like a lotus
Sits on India,
Waiting for the truth
To take him home,
And India
Is busy
Getting busier,
Trying to repay its World Bank Loan.

The Sadhu
Takes his ganja
Like a Rastaman,
He blesses it
And burns it
For the nation,
And as the smoke arrives
In central Pakistan,
The Sadhu talks to God
In meditation.

One day
They say
Gods will return to India,
And all our mixed up lives
Will fall in place,
But first the Gods
Must deal with Bombay's Mafia,
And the Mafia
Control a lot of space.

A Sadhu
Like a lotus
Sits on India,
Waiting for the truth
To take him home,
He's a pure
And dedicated
Meditator,
He's just meditating
With his mobile phone.

FILM: Brunel University, 15 March 2012
POEM: *Propa Propanganda* (Bloodaxe Books, 1996)

Rong Radio

My ears are battered and burned and I have just learned
that I have been listening to the wrong radio station.

My mind has been brutalised now the pain can't be disguised
I've been listening to the wrong radio station.

I was beginning to believe that all black men were bad men
and white men would reign again
I was beginning to believe that I was a mindless drugs freak
that I couldn't control my sanity or my sexuality
I was beginning to believe that I could not believe in nothing
except nothing
and all I ever wanted to do was to get you and to do you.
I've been listening to the wrong radio station.

My future has been blighted I am so short-sighted
I've been listening to the wrong radio station.

I was beginning to not trust me, in fact, I wanted to arrest me
I've been listening to the wrong radio station.

I've been dancing to music that I can't stand.
I've been reciting commercials to my girlfriends.
I've been trying to convince myself that what I really need
is a sunbed and a mortgage and some hairspray,
the kind of hairspray that will wash my grey blues away.

I've been trying to convince myself that I should care about anyone else
but myself
I've been trying to convince myself that could ease my conscience
if I gave a few pence or a few cents to a starving baby in Africa
because African babies need me so
because African babies need my favours
because Africa is full of dictators
and oh yeah globalisation will bring salvation!
I've been listening to the wrong radio station.

I thought my neighbours formed an axis of evil
I wanna go kill people
I've been listening to the wrong radio station.

I am sure I didn't inhale so why is my mind going stale
I've been listening to the wrong radio station.

I was beginning to believe that all Muslims are terrorists
and Christian terrorists think they existed.
I really did believe that terrorism couldn't be done by governments
not our government, not white government,
I just could not see what was wrong with me.
I gave hungry people hamburgers you see.
I was beginning to believe that our children
were better than their children
their children would dying from terrorism
but I couldn't hear their children call
and a child from Palestine simply didn't count at all.
What despair,
no children I was not aware
I'd been listening to the wrong radio station.

For years I've been sedated, and now I think I'm educated.
I've been listening to the wrong radio station
and every time I got ill, I took the same little white pill
I've been listening to the wrong radio station.

When it started I was curious but then it got so serious.
It was cool when it began but now I really hate Iran
and look at me now I wanna make friends with Pakistan.
I wanna bomb Afghanistan, and I need someone to tell me,
where the hell is Kurdistan?
Yeah, you can be my ally for a while until I come to bomb your child
and I'm sure there's a continent called the Middle East
and I think I can bomb my way to peace
I've been listening to the wrong radio station.

I've been listening to the wrong jams,
I've been listening to the wrong beats
I've been listening to the wrong radio station.
I've been listening to the wrong tones of the wrong zones
I've been listening to the wrong radio station.
I've been listening to the wrong voices
I made such mad choices
I've been listening to the wrong radio station.
I've been listening to spies, I've been listening to lies
I've been listening to the wrong radio station.

I needed to know what some pop star somewhere was having for breakfast
I needed to know that I was no longer working class
I needed to know if the stock market rose 1 percent
I needed to know that I had a ruler to give me confidence
I needed to know that my life would improve loads
if I had an operation on my nose.
I needed to hear that DJ say,
'Good morning, good morning!'
I thought he was there just for me
I loved the way that he would say, 'This show was sponsored by...'
'Oh my oh my,' he made me cry
I've been listening to the wrong radio station.

Can you dig this? I put myself on a hit-list
I've been listening to the wrong radio station
I used to take myself for granted
Now I believe I'm wanted
I'm laughing and I'm crying and I'm watching myself dying
I've been listening to the wrong radio station.

Listen to him, can you hear?
Listen to me
Keep this frequency clear!

VIDEO: The Beta Brothers
LYRICS: *Naked* (One Little Indian, 2005)

Football Mad

Oh no, bless my soul
Clever Trevor's scored a goal.

So he runs up the pitch
And wriggles his botty,
He is kissed by ten men
All sweaty and snotty,
Now he's waving his fist
To the Queen who just stares
The lad's going crazy
But everyone cheers.
Now what's he doing?
He's chewing the cud!
Now what's he doing?
He's rolling in mud!
Now he is crying
I think he's in pain
Now what's he doing?
He's smiling again.

Oh no, bless my soul
Clever Trevor's scored a goal.

He's doing gymnastics
He's doing some mime
He's kissing the ground
For a very long time,
With his feet in the air
Now he's gone all religious
And stopped for a prayer.
Did he pray for the sick?
Did he pray for the poor?
No, he prayed for the ball
And he prayed to score.

No one but no one
Can re-start the game
Until Trevor has had
His moment of fame.

Oh, no bless my soul
Clever Trevor's scored a goal,
He kicked the ball into the net
How much money will he get?

FILM: Keats House, 12 October 2011
POEM: *Funky Chickens* (Puffin Books, 1996/1997)

Money

Money mek a rich man feel like a big man
It mek a poor man feel like a hooligan
A one parent family feels like a ruffians
An dose who hav it won't give yu anything,
Money meks yu friend become yu enemy
Yu start see tings very superficially
Yu life is lived very artificially
Unlike dose who live in poverty.
Money inflates yu ego
But money brings yu down
Money causes problems anywea money is found,
Food is what we need, food is necessary,
Mek me grow my food
An dem can eat dem money.

Money meks a singer singaloada crap
Money keeps horses running round de track
Money meks marriages
Money meks divorce
Money meks a student tink about de course,
Money meks commercials
Commercials mek money
If yu don't hav money yu just watch more TV,
Money can save us
But yet we feel doomed,
Plenty money burns ina nuclear mushroom.
Money can't mek yu happy
Money can't help yu when yu die,
It dose who hav it continually live a lie.
Children a dying
Spies a spying
Refugees a fleeing
Politicians a lying,
So deals are done

An webs are spun
Loans keep de Third World on de run,
An de bredda feels betta dan dis bredda next door
Cause dis bredda's got money, and dis bredda's got more
An de bredda tinks dis bredda's not a bredda cause he's poor
When de bredda kills de odder
Dat is economic war.

Economic war
We call it economic war
It may not be de East an de West anymore
But de North an de South
Third World fall out
Coffee an oil is what it's about
It's economic war
Poor people hav de scar
Shots fired from de stock market floor,
So we work fe a living, how we try
An we try,
Wid so little time fe chilling
Like we living a lie.

Money meks a dream become reality
Money meks real life like a fantasy
Money has a habit of going to de head
I have some fe a rainy day underneath me bed,
Money problems mek it hard fe relax
Money meks it difficult to get down to de facts
Money meks yu worship vanity an lies
Money is a drug wid legal eyes
Economists cum
Economists go
Yu try controlling yu cash flow
Food cost loads
An ju juss can't score
An de rich people try to dress like de poor,

Nobody really understands de interest rate
When dere is interest den it's all too late,
We cherish education
But how much do we pay?
Yu can't buy race relations or afford a holiday
Money can't mek yu happy, money can't help yu when you die
An dose who have it continually live a lie.

And now dem sey it's money culture time
Money culture dem, not yours or mine
Money culture who?
Money culture what?
Money culture thrives where luv is not,
Dem can buy an sell until dem gu to Hell
Dem can tax de wisher at de wishing well,
Now Frankenstein cum to privatise
Empire fools, get penny wise.
Every government will tek what dem can get
Every government is quick to forget
Every government can mek money by killing
Every government luvs money, no kidding,
But money is paper an paper will burn
So tink about trees as yu earn,
It could do good but it does more bad
Money is fake and
We've been had.

Some study how to manage it
Some study how to spend it
Some people jus cannot comprehend it
Some study how to move it from one country to another
Some study how to study it an dem study fe ever,
Some people never see it an dem work hard
Other never see it dem juss carry cards,
Some people will grab it without nu thanks
An den mek it pile up in high street banks.

Parents are hoping,
Some are not coping,
Some are jus managing,
Books need balancing,
Property is theft,
Nu money means death,
Yu pay fe yu rent den nothing left,
Some will pick a pocket
Some are paid to stop it
Dose who are paid to stop it are happy
Cause dey got it,
Some gu out an fight for it
Some claim dem hav de right to it
And people like me granparents live long but never sight it.
Money made me gu out an rob
Den it made me gu looking fe a job,
Money made de nurse an de doctor immigrate
Money buys friends yu luv to hate,
Money made slavery seem all right
Money brought de Bible an de Bible shone de light,
Victory to de penniless at grass roots sources
We come to mass down market forces,
Dat paper giant called market forces.

FILM: Live Theatre, Newcastle, 15 March 2009
POEM: *City Psalms* (Bloodaxe Books, 1992)

Talking Turkeys!!

Be nice to yu turkeys dis christmas
Cos turkeys jus wanna hav fun
Turkeys are cool, an turkeys are wicked
An every turkey has a Mum.
Be nice to yu turkeys dis christmas,
Don't eat it, keep it alive,
It could be yu mate an not on yu plate
Say, Yo! Turkey I'm on your side.

I got lots of friends who are turkeys
An all of dem fear christmas time,
Dey wanna enjoy it, dey say humans destroyed it
An humans are out of dere mind,
Yeah, I got lots of friends who are turkeys
Dey all hav a right to a life,
Not to be caged up an genetically made up
By any farmer an his wife.

Turkeys jus wanna play reggae
Turkeys jus wanna hip-hop
Havey you ever seen a nice young turkey saying,
'I cannot wait for de chop'?
Turkeys like getting presents, dey wanna watch christmas TV,
Turkeys hav brains an turkeys feel pain
In many ways like yu an me.

I once knew a turkey called Turkey
He said 'Benji explain to me please,
Who put de turkey in christmas
An what happens to christmas trees?'
I said, 'I am not too sure turkey
But it's nothing to do wid Christ Mass
Humans get greedy and waste more dan need be
An business men mek loadsa cash.'

So, be nice to yu turkey dis christmas
Invite dem indoors fe sum greens
Let dem eat cake an let dem partake
In a plate of organic grown beans,
Be nice to yu turkey dis christmas
An spare dem de cut of de knife,
Join Turkeys United an dey'll be delighted
An yu will mek new friends 'FOR LIFE'.

FILM: Keats House, 12 October 2011
POEM: *Talking Turkeys* (Puffin Books, 1994/1995)

To Do Wid Me

There's a man beating him wife
De woman juss lost her life
Dem called dat domestic strife?
Wot has dat gotta do wid me?

Babies are buried under floors
In a church behind closed doors
I don't know de bloody cause
Wot has dat gotta do wid me?

I've seen all de documentaries
An there's nothing I can do
I've listened to de commentaries
Why should I listen to you?
If I am told to I go vote
If I need more money I strike
If I'm told not to then I won't
I want de best deal out of life

De fit cannot go jogging
Coz there's someone out there mugging
When they should be spreading luving
Wot has dat gotta do wid me?

You an me must juss stand back
Coz they're gonna bomb Iraq
It's a surgical attack so
Wot has dat gotta do wid me?

I juss wanna live my life mate
So juss leave me alone
Why should I fight de state?
When I'm trying to buy my home,
I juss wanna earn my bread guy

An feed my family
You may starve and you may die
But wot has dat gotta do wid me?

Poets are dying in Nigeria
Or forced to leave de area
Multinationals are superior
Wot has dat gotta do wid me?

An in somewherestan I've heard
Dat she can't say a word
An he must grow a beard
Wot has dat gotta do wid me?

Wot has dis gotta do wid me
I'm juss dis guy from Birmingham
An all I want to do is live good in de hood,
It's got nothing to do wid me
I'm juss your average football fan
An hey sum foreign teams are very, very good,
Why should you worry yourself?
You cannot change a single thing
All you gotta do is tek wot you can get,
Why should you worry yourself?
Try hard an you will die trying
Wot can any of us do about Tibet?

I see a million refugees
On twenty million TVs
An I think who de fuck are these?
Wot has dat gotta do wid me?

Hurry up I've got no time
Don't you mess wid wot is mine
Yes I signed de dotted line but
Wot has dat gotta do wid me?

Your school has juss been closed down
Your tax is buying bombs
An although you come from downtown
You don't know where you're coming from,
You don't know wot you are eating
Your food has a terrible taste
An you can be sure dat you are drinking
Sum kinda chemical waste

There's a price upon your head
Even though you're newly wed
A police juss shot you dead
Wot has dat gotta do wid me?

An down in de police station
They are killing de black nation
But dat's normal race relations
Wot has dat gotta do wid me?

Wot has dat gotta do wid
De man upon de corner dat is selling guns
So we can kill each other as we rave,
Or de crackhead who is trying to crack up everyone
Teking all your cash as you become a slave,
Or de mother in de gutter who is begging bread
Where de man dressed in de Gucci hails a cab,
All I am trying to do is praise de Lord it must be said
Wot has dis to do wid anything I've had

A baby in Pakistan
Is making footballs for de man
Or is she an Indian?
Wot has dat gotta do wid me?

There's no propa propaganda
About Malawi or Rwanda
An all dis makes me wonder
Wot has dat gotta do wid me?

I used to go on demonstrations
Now me feet can't tek de pace,
I've tried be a vegan
But there's egg upon me face,
My last stand was de Miners Strike
I did de cop patrol,
Now it's central heating dat I like
An I juss don't need no coal

Indonesia needs more
British arms for East Timor
More western bombs to bomb de poor
Wot has dat gotta do wid me?

An over in Algeria
They say there's another massacre
Isn't dat a part of Africa
Wot has dat gotta do wid me?

An I don't plan to go
To an American death row
There's no compassion there I know but
Wot has dat gotta do wid me?

My God, I can see you have been tortured
An your wife has been drawn an quartered
An your children have been slaughtered
But wot has dat gotta do wid me?

FILM: Custard Factory, Birmingham, 17 July 2012
POEM: *Too Black Too Strong* (Bloodaxe Books, 2001)

Nu Run Away

Black people nu run away
We hav fe stand and fight fe another day.
My people nu run away
We hav fe stand and fight them anyway.

Dem have a little power
An now dem want devour
De disabled, single parents and de Blacks.
Dem sey dem spending money
In a bid to mek you happy
But de truth is dat you just cannot relax.
Dem sey you hav a share
But you can't can't see it anywhere
Dem set up a lottery to fool de nation.
Dem nah deal wid charity
An de black reality
Is every week a brother dead ina de station.

Black people nu run away
we hav fe stand and fight fe another day.
My people nu run away
We hav fe stand and fight them anyway.

Dem talk bout equal opportunities
In schools and universities
Now dem hav a brand new scheme,
Play your drum, do sum sport
But an intellectual thought means
A uniform removes you from de scene,
An a priest on TV
Representing you and me
Tells de world that he cyant understand.
Well to put it simply
There is no equality
An equality is what people demand.

CHORUS
Black people nu run away
we hav fe stand and fight fe another day.
Stand firm.
My people nu run away
We hav fe stand and fight them anyway.

Stand firm.
You got yu colour TV.
Stand firm.
But dat don't mean you are free.
Stand firm.
Even if yu wages mek yu sweet.
Stand firm.
It is no good if yu cannot walk de streets.
Mek dem move yah,
Gu wea yah,
I am tell you we hav fe stick together
Mek dem move yah
Back wea yah
And beware of de
New World Order.
Mek dem move yah,
Gu wea yah
Mek dem know dat we have ways of fighting back
Mek dem move yah,
Back wea yah
Zephaniah and Professor tell yu dat.

CHORUS
Don't turn.
CHORUS

FILM: Custard Factory, Birmingham, 17 July 2012
MUSIC & LYRICS: *Belly of De Beast* (Ariwa Music, 1996)

BONUS FEATURE

MUSIC VIDEOS

Us an Dem

Me hear dem a talk bout Unity
Dem hav a plan fe de Effnick Minority
Dem sey Liberation totally
But dem hav odder tings as priority.
Dem hold a Conference anually
Fe look at de state of Equality
Dem claim dem fighting hard fe we
When we want do it Independently,
De us,
Dat's dose who are made fe suffer
Some are found in de gutter wid no food fe eat,
Us,
Well, we are clearly frustrated
We jus not debated when Parliament meet,
Dem,
Well dey are known by dere fruits
Dem hav many troops fe batter yu down,
Dem,
Well, now dem hav power
But dere shall be an hour
When de table turn round.

Us an Dem it is Us an Dem
When will dis ting ever end
Yu mus know yu enemy from yu fren

Know yu enemy from yu fren now
Face de facts, yu can't pretend now,
I write dis poem fe more dan Art
I live a struggle, de poem plays a part,
I know people, very trendy
Dem talk to me very friendly,
But dey are coping
So now dem voting all dem frens in,

De frens oppress we,
How dem oppress we?
Well dem arrest we
An den dem givin we Judge an Jury
When we start we demonstrating
Dem hav dem prison cell waiting,
Pon de Telly dem talk fe a while
Wid fancy words an dem plastic smile,
Where Party Politricks play its tricks
Dere is nu luv fe de old, nu luv fe de sick.

Us an Dem it is Us an Dem.

Now me hear dem a talk bout World Peace,
But dere's Wars at home
An dem Wars will not cease,
Not till all de Queen horses
Women an Men find a new direction
(Start again),
Politicians talk 'bout World economics,
But read de Manifesto
It reads like a comic,
When dem talk bout housing
Dem mouth start sprouting
Words dat fe ever an fe ever yu doubting,
If yu in doubt yu don't hav a shout
When yu talk against dem
Dem sey get out,
Some call it Democracy
I call it Hypocrisy
Dat mek me start feel Revolutionary,
When rich fashion cramps poor style
I stop an after a while I ask,
Is it me class or is it me colour
Or is it a ting I don't yet discover,

Us an Dem it is Us an Dem
When will dis ting ever end,
Us an Dem it is Us an Dem.

Yu mus know yu enemy from yu fren,
I repeat again, now it's Us an Dem,
When will dis ting reach a conclusion,
Don't pretend are yu Us or Dem,
Pick yu place from now
Before de confusion.

VIDEO: Mango Island
POEM: *City Psalms* (Bloodaxe Books, 1992)

Touch

When I see you I know life was made for living
When I see you I don't wanna die
When I don't see you I sleep and dream about you
It's the truth I'm telling you, poets don't lie.
Sometimes I think I can't survive without you
I wanna introduce you to my crew
Sometimes I think I wanna give it all up
Everything, well, everything but you.

When I see you I know life is about sharing
When I see you I know why the caged bird sings
When I see you I know why it is I'm caring
About love and life and every living thing.
And now that we are in this space together
And the party people have all come and gone
I really want this time to last forever
So I'm asking you to keep your clothing on.

Yeah I wanna touch your body
Yeah I wanna touch your body
Yeah I wanna touch your body
But first I wanna touch your mind.

When I look upon your face I feel inspired
I feel a loving surge when I get close to you
It's intelligence that I really admire
That is why I like to think things through.
You light me up when darkness falls upon me
You cool me when I cannot take the heat
I feel so wanted anytime you call me
Even though you kinda knock me off my feet.
And when you smile it's like the sun is shining
And all the good around me seems to grow.

Yeah girl you got the rhythm and the timing
So let's take things nice and slow.
Check out that we're dancing to the same tune
Check where we're going to and coming from
And the seeds that we have planted will blossom soon
But girl keep your clothing on.

Yeah I wanna touch your body
Yeah I wanna touch your body
Yeah I wanna touch your body
But first I wanna touch your mind.

I wanna touch you girl. Right in your head.
I wanna touch you girl. Deeper, deeper.
I wanna touch you girl. Right in your head.
I wanna touch you girl. Deeper, deeper.

I wanna touch you girl. Right in your head.
I wanna touch you girl. Deeper, deeper.
I wanna touch you girl. Right in your head.
I wanna touch you girl. Deeper, deeper.

It's emotional, it's spiritual, it's natural
Our union is something to behold
But we can't afford to keep it superficial
Cause it's all about the body and the soul
I reckon that this trip could last forever
But nothing must be done with any force
Let's put our minds together
And have mental intercourse

Yeah I wanna touch your body
Yeah I wanna touch your body
Yeah I wanna touch your body
But first I wanna touch your mind

I wanna touch you girl. Right in your head.
I wanna touch you girl. Deeper, deeper.
I wanna touch you girl. Right in your head.
I wanna touch you girl. Deeper, deeper.

Deeper, deeper.

VIDEO: The Beta Brothers
LYRICS: *Naked* (One Little Indian, 2005)

Responsible

Sey what is going on down ina Babylon
You can't blame unemployment every time yu rong
Sey what is going on down in de ghetto man
Every time yu children need yu man yu come and gone,
Sey what is going on, what's doing in yu head
Your sister said de situation kinda dread
All tings are possible, but to be credible
My brother man yu gotta be responsible.

CHORUS
Brother you gotta be responsible
Brother yu gotta get in touch wid yu senses
Brother you gotta be responsible
And when yu do stuff yu mus face de consequences,
Brother you gotta be responsible
If necessary brother I will contradict yu
Brother you gotta be responsible
To be a man yu gotta respect yu sister.

Your sister ain't a bitch, nu matter how yu rich
Yu gotta find some positive communication,
If you're so limited, yu gotta deal wid it
Because your sister is de mother of creation,
Your sister ain't a hoe, de prophet said so
Yu better check yu history and let yu knowledge grow,
So what yu saying now, I gotta let yu know
Dat unity is cool and dat's the way to go.

CHORUS

Listen brother man what's going on
Yu gotta be responsible
Listen brother man what's going on
Den anything is possible.

So listen brother man what's going on
Yu really don't know what will happen next
Listen brother man yu gotta cum around
Yu gotta show some respect.

What kinda man are you, what so you plan to do,
If yu bigging up yu self then don't be shallow,
If you have a clue then you will know it's true
Yu can't blame all yu sins on de ghetto.
So don't come size me up, let us rise up
Cause when the truth come there will be no where to hide
De system is corrupt but if yu getting fired up
Yu gotta make sure that your sisters at your side.

Get in touch with your senses
Face the consequences
You gotta be responsible
All things are possible.

VIDEO: The Beta Brothers
LYRICS: *Naked* (One Little Indian, 2005)

Genetics

You get drunk without drinking
And your grass is turning red
You wonder without thinking
There's a mushroom in your head.
Your kids don't recognise you
You don't recognise yourself
You're trying to get to know you
But you're knowing someone else.
Your water has been pasteurised
Your pets are in control
The children in the nursery
Are looking very old.
Cows are giving birth to donkeys
And those donkeys will soon fly
There's a member of your family
That you can't identify.
It's all about genetics.

Your hand has grown a foot
And you cannot get a head
And you believe it when you're told
That you're very good in bed.
You cannot grow your rice
Because there's something in the clay
When you went to eat your supper
Your supper just walked away.
This is madness but this madness
Is the best money can buy
This madness brings forth great sadness
But you can't afford to cry.
There's a baby in the bottle
Plutonium in your perm
There's no power in your throttle
But there's acid in your sperm.
It's all about genetics.